● Finger Holes Closed
○ Finger Holes Open

(Numbers) Left Hand Keys
(Letters) Right Hand Keys

BOEHM SY

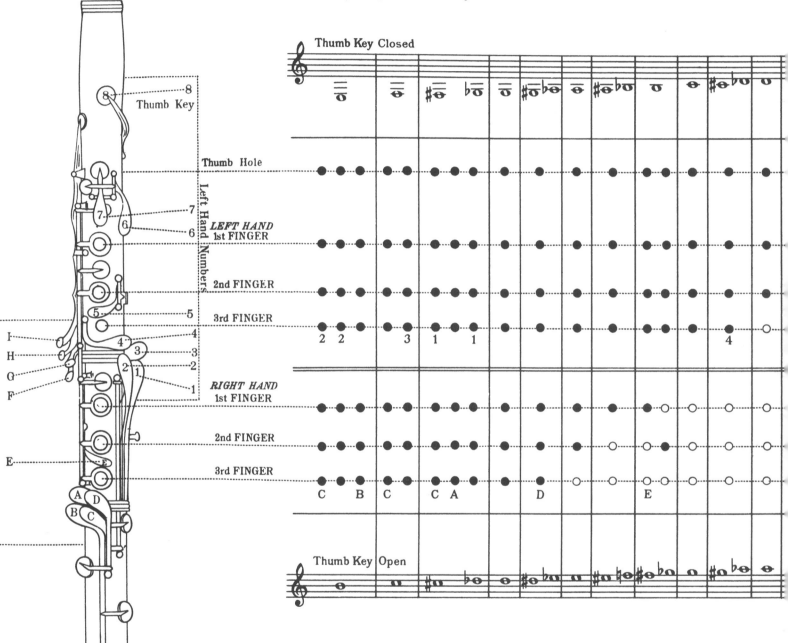

RUBANK
STEM CLARINET CHART

By ROBERT MILLER

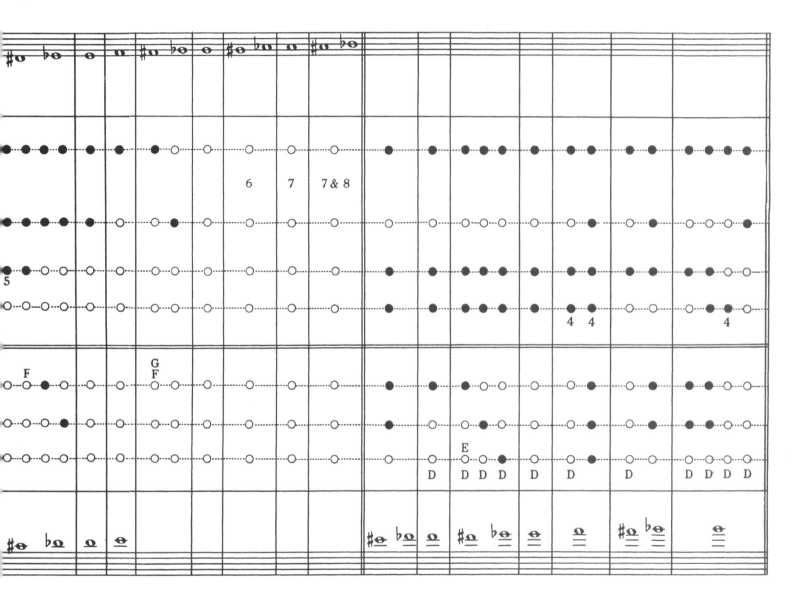

RUBANK Elementary METHOD

CLARINET

N. W. HOVEY

A FUNDAMENTAL COURSE FOR INDIVIDUAL
OR LIKE-INSTRUMENT CLASS INSTRUCTION

HAL•LEONARD®

LESSON 1

Whole Notes—Whole Rests

N. W. HOVEY

★ T 1 means Thumb Hole and 1st Finger Hole are covered.
   T 2 means Thumb Hole and 1st & 2nd Finger Holes are covered, etc.

Half Notes – Half Rests

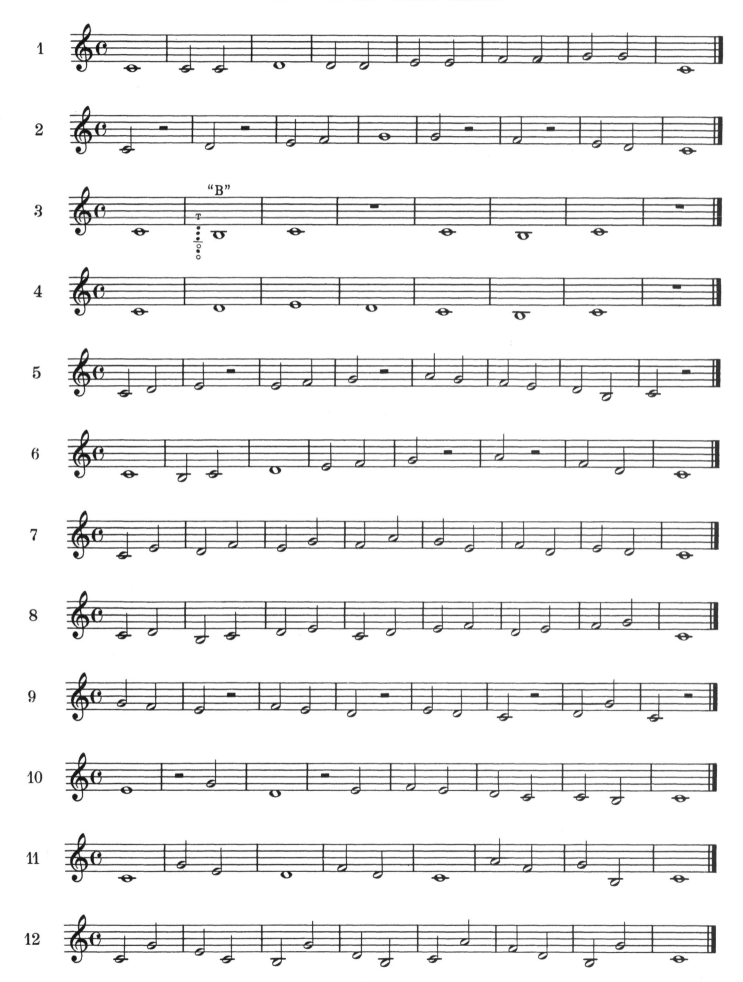

Quarter Notes – Quarter Rests

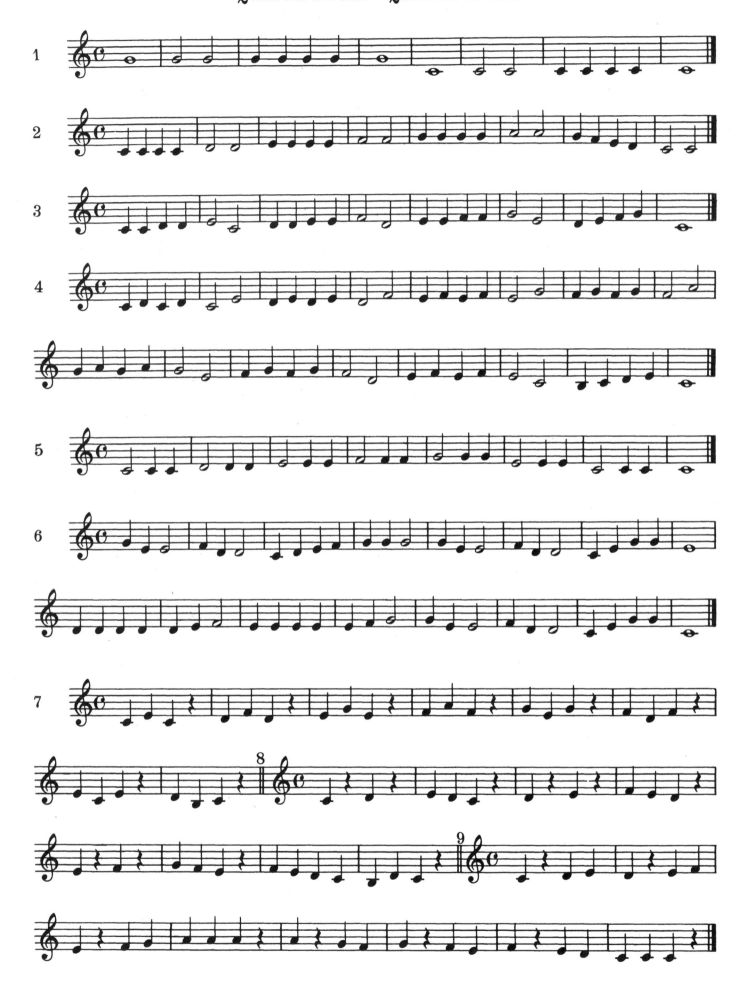

Quarter Notes (Continued)

The Tie; Dotted Half Notes

Eighth Notes

Key of F (Eighths Continued)

"B flat"

(Eighths Continued)

* O.K. &
A Key

"B flat"

* O.K. means Octave Key

Use All Melody Band Folio by Davis for Unison playing, for full band.

Rubank Elem. Clar. Meth.

Dotted Quarter Notes

ALWAYS NOTE THE KEY-SIGNATURE
CAREFULLY BEFORE PLAYING AN EXERCISE.

Three Quarter Time

An interesting Solo at this stage is Cradle Song by Brahms (entirely in low register). Contained in Radio Collection of Modern Gems for Bb Clarinet and Piano.

Upper Register

* O.K. means Octave (Register) Key.

The Register Change

REFER to SUPPLEMENTARY TUNES
WHEN THIS LESSON HAS BEEN COMPLETED.

Abide With Me

Wm. H. Monk

Blue Bells of Scotland

Scotch Folk Song

Andante Moderato

The First Noel

Traditional

Moderato

Come, All Ye Faithful

Traditional

Grandioso

Intervals On the Register Change

Eighth Notes On the Register Change

Eighth Rests, On and Off Beat

Rhythmic patterns to be practiced. Repeat each measure several times.

Alla Breve (cut time)

Key of B♭ (Alla Breve Continued)

*) On changes from C to E♭ or E♭ to C, play C with little finger of LEFT hand.
Ask your instructor or consult fingering chart.

Alla Breve, Quarter Rests On and Off Beat

★ High B♭ fingered with first finger of each hand (in B♭ major chord and any change from F to B♭) Boehm system clarinets.

Six-Eight Time

Practice the next three lessons beating *six* to a measure, emphasizing or slightly accenting counts 1 and 4 (1 2 3 4 5 6).

Then review all three lessons beating *two* to a measure, so that the first beat falls on count 1 and the second beat on count 4.

An interesting Solo at this stage is Barcarolle by Offenbach, arranged by H.W. Davis for Bb Clarinet and Piano.

Six-Eight Time

*   B♮ in this case is called an "accidental" because the key *signature* calls for a B♭. An accidental affects all like notes within that measure *only*.

Six Eight-Time

REFER to SUPPLEMENTARY TUNES
WHEN THIS LESSON HAS BEEN COMPLETED

Drink to Me Only With Thine Eyes

English Air

1 Andante moderato

There is a Green Hill Far Away

Geo. C. Stebbins

2 Moderato

Believe Me, If All Those Endearing Young Charms

Moore

3 Moderato

Silent Night, Holy Night

Franz Gruber

4 Moderato

The Slur

Staccato

crescendo (gradually louder)

f (loud)

f

diminuendo (gradually softer)

p (softly)

p

p

1st ending   2nd ending

Key of Eb

Review of Keys

Sixteenth Notes

(See footnote on counting)

down beat | up beat

↓ | ↑

one | and

one - da | an - da

Sixteenth Notes

(See footnote on counting)

Sixteenth Notes

(See footnote on counting)

Key of G

Dotted Eighths Followed By Sixteenths

REFER to SUPPLEMENTARY TUNES
WHEN THIS LESSON HAS BEEN COMPLETED

An interesting Solo at this stage is Nocturne by Mendelssohn, arranged by H.W. Davis for B♭ Clarinet and Piano.

Key of D

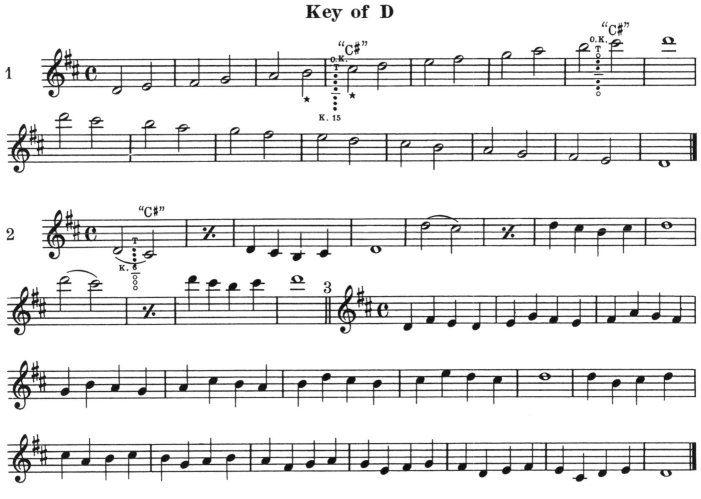

★ There are different ways of playing B and C sharp in scales of two sharps and over. Learn all fingerings and sharp scales will be easier to play.

Key of A

★ Use same fingering as in Lesson 31.

Review of Sharp Keys

R — indicates little finger of right hand.
L — indicates little finger of left hand.

Additional Rhythmic Figures in Alla Breve

Chromatic

At this point it is advisable for the pupil to practice and memorize the preceding exercise in whole notes, halves, quarters, and eighths.

★) Consult Boehm fingering chart or ask your instructor.

Key 5

Chromatic

★ See note bottom of Lesson 35

An interesting Solo at this stage is To April by Gene Paul for Bb Clarinet and Piano.

Syncopation

REFER to SUPPLEMENTARY TUNES
WHEN THIS LESSON HAS BEEN COMPLETED

America, the Beautiful

Samuel A. Ward

Aloha Oe

Queen Liliuakalaui

Come Back to Erin

C. Barnard

Major Chords

Phrasing for chord studies.

Sustained Tones for Daily Practice

✱ Refer to Lesson 18 for proper fingering of high B♭ in chord.

Melody

SCHUMANN

Moderato semplice, ♩ = 104

p

*This number can be had for Two Clarinets and Piano, arranged by H.W. Davis. Price 60 cents.

Annie Laurie

Scotch Melody

Andante con moto, ♩ = 84

p (Melody)

Gavotte

GOSSEC

Allegretto, ♩=76

Battle Hymn of the Republic

♩=104

Hunters Chorus

WEBER

Duet From Lucia

DONIZETTI

Melody from the Opera Orpheus

Andante, ♩ = 69

GLUCK

*This number can be had for Two B♭ Clarinets with Piano Acc. under the title of Spirit Dance from Orpheus, arranged by H. W. Davis.

Gob Sticks

WEBER